WHY BUY QUANTRILL'S BONES?

by

Gail B. Stewart

Illustrated by
James Watling

CRESTWOOD HOUSE
NEW YORK

Maxwell Macmillan Canada
Toronto

Maxwell Macmillan International
New York   Oxford   Singapore   Sydney

Library of Congress Cataloging-in-Publication Data
Stewart, Gail, 1949-

Why buy Quantrill's Bones? / by Gail B. Stewart. — 1st ed.
    p.   cm. — (History's mysteries)
Includes bibliographical references and index.
ISBN 0-89686-614-9
1. Quantrill, William Clarke, 1837-1865—Relics. 2. Missouri—History—Civil War, 1861-1865. 3.
Kansas—History—Civil War, 1861-1865. I. Title II. Series.
    E470.45.Q3S74 1992
    973.7'092—dc20
    [B]   91-23120
                                                                                                  CIP
                                                                                                   AC

Copyright © 1992 Crestwood House, Macmillan Publishing Company

Crestwood House
Macmillan Publishing Company
866 Third Avenue
New York, NY 10022

Maxwell Macmillan Canada, Inc.
1200 Eglinton Avenue East
Suite 200
Don Mills, Ontario M3C 3N1

Macmillan Publishing Company is part of the Maxwell Communication Group of Companies.

First edition

Printed in the United States of America

10 9 8 7 6 5 4 3 2 1

CONTENTS

▲▲▲▲▲▲▲▲▲▲▲▲▲▲▲▲▲▲▲▲▲▲▲▲▲▲▲▲▲

THE CASE OPENS

▲▲▲▲▲▲▲▲▲▲▲▲▲▲▲▲▲▲▲▲▲▲▲▲▲▲▲▲▲▲▲▲

He was only 27 years old when he died.

His name was William Quantrill, and he and his "raiders" had been hunted by Union soldiers for more than two years. He himself wore the blue uniform of the Union side in the Civil War, but it was only a disguise. He was a Confederate, he said, for he hated the North.

On the morning of May 10, 1865, Quantrill and eleven of his men were hiding out at a farm outside Louisville, Kentucky, owned by James Wakefield. Wakefield had given them permission to hide there. Under the cold, pelting rain, Quantrill's men had little to do. Some napped in the barn. Others outside threw corncobs back and forth in a mock battle.

A squadron of Union soldiers had heard rumors that Quantrill was in the area. They tracked him to

Wakefield's farm. As they approached, Quantrill's men began firing.

Quantrill was sleeping in the hayloft when he heard the first shots. He ran from the barn, leading his horse. He tried to swing himself into the saddle, but the gunfire frightened his horse. The animal wouldn't stand still long enough for Quantrill to mount.

So Quantrill ran through the muddy barnyard toward the woods. He was shot twice from behind—once in the hand, once in the back.

His back wound paralyzed him from the shoulders down. He was bleeding heavily. Some Union soldiers carried him inside Wakefield's house and laid him on a bed.

The next day he was moved to a military hospital in Louisville. The raiders not killed in the shootout surrendered to the Union army. Some of them came to pay their respects to Quantrill before he died on June 6, 1865.

Historian Paul Wellman wrote in *A Dynasty of Western Outlaws* that there was an "especially unpleasant aftermath" to Quantrill's death.

Quantrill was buried in a Catholic cemetery in Louisville in 1865. His family, who lived in Ohio, did not request that he be buried in the family plot, perhaps because William had fought against the North. Ohio was a Northern state.

Twenty years later, Quantrill's mother asked a family friend, W. W. Scott, to locate her son's grave and bring his remains back to Ohio. Scott did as he was asked. According to Wellman, Scott gave the cemetery employee a few dollars to put the bones in a box. These were turned over to Mrs. Quantrill.

But instead of reburying her son's remains, Mrs. Quantrill sold them! According to Scott's diary, "Mrs. Q afterwards had the lot sold and received the money." It is not known who bought the bones, or for what price.

Why would anybody buy them?

THE CASE FILE

▲▲▲▲▲▲▲▲▲▲▲▲▲▲▲▲▲▲▲▲▲▲▲▲▲▲▲▲▲▲▲▲▲

NORTHERN BEGINNINGS

When Quantrill died, one Kansas newspaper carried the headline: "The Monster Is Dead." Was he a monster? Many people say he was. Others say that Quantrill was only a ruthless soldier who happened to fight for the side that lost the Civil War. However Quantrill is judged, one thing is clear—his name is legendary in American history.

Quantrill is so well-known for his bloody battles against the North that one might think he was a native Southerner. In fact, he was not. The oldest of 14 children, he was born and raised in Canal Dover, Ohio.

Historians say that as a child William Quantrill was a bully. He enjoyed picking on children smaller than himself. He also like nailing snakes to trees, killing small dogs and whipping cows and horses.

According to Carl Breihan in *Quantrill and His Civil War Raiders*, Quantrill's favorite form of cruelty was to torture two cats. He would "tie their tails together and hang them over a wire fence or clothesline, and watch them claw and fight frantically until both were dead." Cruelty, wrote Breihan, was "a part of Quantrill's nature."

He got into a lot of trouble around town. Eventually, William's mother sent him with another family that was planning to travel to Illinois. She hoped the change would be good for him.

Unfortunately, trouble seemed to follow William Quantrill. He left Illinois after being accused of murder. The sheriff was sure he had done it, but no witnesses could be found so Quantrill was released. His lawyer did advise him, however, to leave the state.

ALIAS CHARLEY HART

Mrs. Quantrill heard little from William over the next several years. He moved to Indiana, then to Kansas. In Kansas he tried farming for a while, but found it dull. He left after a winter during which his neighbors mysteriously lost blankets, food and other necessities. According to Carl Breihan, "finally they . . . caught Quantrill in the act of

plundering one of their cabins. Quantrill changed his name to Charley Hart and left the settlement."

In 1858 Quantrill was in the army and traveling west on an expedition. He was part of a wagon train taking supplies to a regiment stationed in Utah. He stayed out west. For a while it seemed that he had found a place he enjoyed.

Then Quantrill was told to leave the army. Some accounts suggest he was stealing again. Other sources claim he was operating illegal gambling games.

Whichever story was true, Quantrill returned to Kansas. The law in Kansas had urged him to stay out of the state years before, but with his new name, "Charley" was sure he could make a fresh start.

But he was returning to an area gripped by brutal, bloody fighting. Soon, Quantrill would make the fighting even bloodier.

A TROUBLING QUESTION

As William Quantrill was making his way back to Kansas, the United States was wrestling with a difficult question. Was slavery right or wrong? The question divided people.

Most Southerners believed slavery was good. They supported slavery because their economy depended on it. Large plantations of peanuts, fruit and cotton could not produce large and inexpensive crops without free slave labor.

Many Northerners were against slavery. They felt it was wrong for one person to own another. Unlike the South, the North did not depend on slaves to make their economy work. The North was more industrially based. Because the northern economy could afford to pay a labor force, their position was based on ideas of right and wrong, not on dollars and cents.

The slavery question divided Congress as well. Northern leaders wanted slavery abolished; southern leaders wanted to keep it. What would be the policy of new states and territories? Would settlers be allowed to own slaves?

In 1854 Congress had agreed on a plan. Known as "popular sovereignty," the plan called for each new territory to make up its own mind. If settlers wanted slavery, they could decide that by a vote.

The same year, Congress passed the Kansas-Nebraska Act opening these two new territories to settlers. The slavery question in these territories was uncertain. Nebraska was fairly far to the north, and few settlers were attracted there. It was unlikely that slaves would be needed or wanted there.

But Kansas was a different story.

KANSAS IN THE MIDDLE

Part of the trouble was that Kansas was bordered to the east by Missouri. At that time, Missouri was the state farthest west. The land west of Missouri was still open territory. For decades it had been the last stop for traders, trappers and those heading west to search for gold. In the many little towns along Missouri's western border, merchants sold food and supplies to the travelers heading west.

Missouri had a thriving economy. But it was a slave state and voted with the South in Congress. Missouri had reason to want Kansas to become a slave state too.

The slavery issue was really about power and control. James Berry wrote in *Bloody Kansas* that slavery was only a convenient rallying cry. North and South "fought each other in Kansas for the added strength that the extra land and the extra votes of that area would bring, once the territory was settled."

Proslavery people in Kansas were strengthened by the nearness of Missouri. The center for the antislavery leaders, who were called abolitionists, was far away in New England. Abolitionists knew

they couldn't influence many Kansans from that far away. Instead, they formed support groups that raised money for abolitionists to settle in Kansas. Sometimes these support groups sent supplies to the Kansas settlers. The supplies included weapons.

POLITICS FAILS TO SOLVE IT

Congress called for an election in Kansas in 1855. The settlers there would elect representatives who would decide whether slavery would be allowed in Kansas.

Those on both sides of the argument felt strongly about it. The proslavery people did not want to leave the election up for grabs. Missouri Senator David Atchison even urged Missouri citizens to cross the border and vote for proslavery candidates! This was illegal, but Atchison was determined that slavery should win out. In a letter to the Secretary of War, Atchison wrote, "We will be compelled to shout, burn, and hang, but the thing will soon be done."

At the time there were 1,500 eligible votes in Kansas. When the votes were counted, officials found that more than 6,000 votes had been cast. The proslavery, southern party won.

The antislavery people demanded a new election. They gathered in the town of Lawrence, Kansas, and drew up a formal condemnation of the new legislature. The new legislators didn't care what the abolitionists thought. They set about passing laws that would make Kansas a slave state. So the abolitionists elected their own legislators, making Lawrence their official headquarters. They passed their own laws making Kansas a free state.

The laws accomplished nothing. Tempers on both sides were hot. There was growing concern that only violence would settle the issue. The country would eventually fight the slavery battle in the Civil War. But five years before that war began, it was fought in Kansas.

"BLEEDING KANSAS"

Rumors that fighting would break out brought people who wanted to get in on the fight to Kansas. The issues of slavery and freedom mattered very little to them.

Proslavery mobs burned down part of Lawrence. Abolitionists, led by John Brown, killed five proslavery people at Pottawatomie Creek west of Lawrence. Attacks from one side were followed by attacks from the other.

At the time Quantrill returned to Kansas, leaders were emerging. The most famous of the antislavery fighters was James Lane. He was known as the "Grim Chieftain of Kansas." Lane led raids across the border into Missouri.

Lane was also a great public speaker. He traveled to various northern states telling people about the horrible situation in "Bleeding Kansas." He was so persuasive that wealthy abolitionists in his audiences contributed money. Most of the money was used to buy weapons and ammunition.

Quantrill became well-known as a soldier in favor of slavery. But briefly, as late as 1858, he was a supporter of the antislavery movement in Kansas.

In *Inside War* historian Michael Fellman included parts of letters Quantrill wrote to his mother from Kansas. Quantrill complained about the lies being told by the proslavery people. He also defended Lane, saying, "He's as good a man as we have."

QUANTRILL IN KANSAS

Quantrill was a schoolteacher in Kansas. Historians say he looked far more like a teacher than a vicious guerrilla fighter. These are independent fighters who often use harassment and subterfuge in warfare.

Quantrill was tall and thin with a boyish face. He

18

could have been handsome, except for his eyes. Those who knew him spoke of his "cold blue eyes" and his "icy stare that could freeze a man's blood." Pictures of Quantrill show that he had very thick, drooping eyelids.

People tended to be uncomfortable around Quantrill. He seemed secretive, even suspicious, and was often alone. Sometimes he said things that people felt were odd. In *Quantrill and His Civil War Guerrillas,* Carl Breihan told about a conversation Quantrill had with a friend. While walking peacefully along a riverbank, Quantrill saw a tree with a large, wide branch. He said to his companion, "I could hang six men on that limb!"

While working as a teacher, Quantrill sometimes participated in raids. Historians agree that at first he played both sides. He stole slaves from Kansas owners and then went into Missouri to sell the slaves there. While in Missouri, he stole horses to sell to settlers in Kansas. Although at the time he claimed to believe in the abolitionist cause, he didn't seem to care that sometimes he worked against it.

AN ODD TURN OF EVENTS

William Quantrill left Kansas for good in 1860, under very strange circumstances.

The situation along the Kansas-Missouri border had become increasingly intense. Angry groups of people from both sides were raiding border towns. Property was damaged and lives were lost.

Quantrill led three abolitionists on a raid into Missouri in December 1860. The purpose was to liberate the slaves of a wealthy farmer named Morgan Walker. But Quantrill secretly warned Walker. Walker and his sons waited with shotguns for Quantrill's party to approach. Without realizing it, the three young abolitionists had let Quantrill lead them into a deadly trap.

Why Quantrill blew the whistle on his own raid has confused historians. Some have speculated that he was romantically involved with Morgan Walker's daughter. They believe Quantrill warned Walker out of loyalty.

Others aren't so sure. They think Quantrill was simply looking for a chance to change sides and become a proslavery Missouri raider. They point out that Quantrill had been banished from Kansas and may have carried a grudge against the state.

The people of Missouri were certainly puzzled. They weren't sure that they could trust this raider from Kansas. They listened when Quantrill told them the reason he'd sabotaged the raid.

He said a group of Kansas abolitionists had killed his older brother. According to Harrison Trow, a close friend of Quantrill's, this happened while Quantrill and his brother were on the way to California. In *A True Story of Chas. W. Quantrill*—remember that Quantrill often used the name Charley—Trow reported Quantrill's account of the murder:

"Upon reaching Little Cottonwood River, Kansas, they decided to camp for the night. . . . All was going well. After supper 21 outlaws . . . belonging to Jim Lane at Lawrence, Kansas, rode up and killed the elder brother, wounded Charles, and took everything in sight.

"They left poor Charles there to die. . . . Poor Charles lay there for 3 days before anyone happened by, guarding his dead brother, suffering near death from his wounds."

The sad tale touched the Missouri settlers who heard it. But they had no way of knowing that the story was a lie. William "Charles" Quantrill never had an older brother!

For whatever reason, as of December 1860 Quantrill had again changed sides in the border war. He had become a proslavery Missouri man.

QUANTRILL'S RAIDERS

The border of Kansas and Missouri had been a hotbed of violence, with loosely knit bands of guerrillas from both sides terrorizing and killing settlers. With the start of the Civil War in 1861, the fighting grew bloodier.

The Kansas guerrillas were known as Jayhawkers or sometimes Red Legs. The guerrillas from Missouri were known as bushwhackers. Both sides were bloodthirsty.

Quantrill soon won a reputation among the bushwhackers as a ruthless soldier. Within a few months of the Morgan Walker incident, he had assembled a group of his own raiders.

Just as when he was on his own, Quantrill and his raiders worked both sides of the border. Their main targets were Union soldiers. They raided Union camps in Kansas and stole horses to sell in Missouri. They kidnapped free black settlers in Kansas and sold them as slaves in Missouri. With this money, the raiders bought ammunition and weapons.

The raiders also looted and robbed settlers in Kansas. Often they grabbed a farmer from his bed, hung him, then robbed his house in the night. Sometimes the looted farm was burned.

Before the war was over, more than 450 men rode with Quantrill's raiders. Some might have wanted to fight for the Confederate army but just didn't fit into the traditional soldier's role. Others had grievances against the Union army. Still others felt cheated by the abolitionists and antislavery Jayhawkers.

Harrison Trow wrote that the Jayhawkers were poor men who robbed and looted out of envy at their Missouri neighbors' slavery-based prosperity. Trow explained the bushwhackers' response to the Jayhawkers' actions by asking a bitter question. "Is it any wonder, then, that the Missourians whose father was killed should kill in return, whose house was burnt should burn in return, whose property was plundered should pillage in return?"

This revengeful attitude was common among Quantrill's guerrillas. Cole Younger, for example, had seen northern raiders force his sick mother to set fire to her own house. He carried that memory into each battle.

Frank James, who along with his younger brother Jesse would later form the notorious James gang, had seen his stepfather hanged by Union soldiers.

Perhaps the most dreaded and feared of all Quantrill's raiders was "Bloody Bill" Anderson. Cold-blooded Anderson proudly hung his victims' scalps from the bridle of his horse.

Anderson had hated the northern soldiers ever since they had arrested his three young sisters. The girls were crowded into a rickety jail in Kansas City with other women who had ties to guerrilla fighters, even though townspeople warned that the jail was unsafe. The jail collapsed in 1861, crushing many of the prisoners. Two of the dead were Anderson's sisters, aged 10 and 18.

"Bloody Bill" vowed to get even and fought more viciously than before. He began keeping a long silk cord in his saddlebag. Whenever he killed a Northerner, he made a knot in the cord. When Anderson was finally killed in an ambush, he had 54 knots in the cord.

So hated was Anderson by the Union army, in fact, that they mocked him after his death. He was propped up with pistols in each hand for a photograph. Then Union soldiers cut off Anderson's head and displayed it on the end of a telegraph pole.

"I HOPE TO GOD THEY WILL BE SHOT"

"Bloody Bill" Anderson was not the only skilled guerrilla fighter in the outfit. Quantrill insisted his men practice shooting for hours each day.

The raiders were outfitted with Colt navy revolvers. They could hit their target either standing or while on a galloping horse. They carried at least two guns so they didn't have to reload as often. Some of the raiders carried eight!

Because they were guerrillas, they did not wear Confederate uniforms. Usually they wore large, loose-fitting shirts with scooped necks. Each shirt had deep pockets for ammunition. Quantrill's raiders took pride in their shirts. Mothers, wives or girlfriends embroidered them or decorated them with beads.

When they weren't wearing these fancy shirts, the guerrillas wore Union uniforms. They stole these or took them from dead northern soldiers. The purpose in this was trickery.

Raiders wearing Union hats and shirts looked like northern soldiers from a distance. This enabled Quantrill and his men to approach patrols of Union soldiers, often getting within point-blank shooting range. They wiped out scores of Union patrols this way.

One soldier wrote in his journal in 1862, "Colonel Boyd has several guerrillas under arrest and I hope to God they will be shot. I hate their getting the clothing worst of all for now we cannot tell them from our own men."

THE BLACK FLAG

Early in the Civil War, Quantrill visited Richmond, Virginia. He wanted to talk Confederate leaders into waging a "black flag" war.

The black flag was a symbol of guerrilla fighters. Anyone fighting under a black flag would take no prisoners and aid no wounded. It was a fight to the death. Killing and destruction were the most important things. Quantrill asked his men to take an oath before they joined his band. As part of the oath, men swore "our purpose is to tear down, lay waste, despoil and kill our enemies. Mercy . . . is no part of a fighter's outfit."

The Confederate officers were uneasy with such ideas. Some were horrified. According to Carl Breihan, the Confederate Secretary of War, James A. Seddon, told Quantrill that "in the nineteenth century it is plain barbarism to talk of a 'black flag.' "

Quantrill also asked that his men be outfitted by

the Confederate army and that he be given the rank of colonel. These requests were denied. When he returned to Missouri, Quantrill was bitter. He would go on fighting, but now with his own army.

AIMING AT LAWRENCE

No act of William Quantrill's is as famous—or infamous—as his attack on Lawrence, Kansas, on August 21, 1863.

For years Lawrence had been the headquarters of the abolitionist movement in Kansas. With a population of 3,000, Lawrence was one of the most prosperous cities in Kansas. It was a recruiting center for the Union army and the home of the northern guerrilla leader James Lane.

Quantrill carefully explained his attack plan to his men. He asked some of his key fighters what they thought.

Unanimously, the men wanted to attack Lawrence. Carl Breihan wrote that after each man's name was called, he made comments like "Burn Lawrence to the ground!"

Three hundred men rode out with Quantrill from Blackwater River in Johnson County in western Missouri. Along the way they were joined by another 150 men. Many carried lists of people in Lawrence they wished to kill or torture. At the top of Quantrill's list was James Lane.

The men rode for two days and nights. They made few stops. Many of them slept as they rode, using belts or ropes to tie themselves to their saddles.

Several times when the raiders were in unfamiliar territory, they stopped to ask a farmer to guide them. Each time, after the farmer had guided them some distance, the raiders shot him in the back of the head.

Soon they neared Lawrence, reaching the farms and homes of people on their lists near sunrise. The guerrillas' signal was a single pistol shot from Quantrill himself. On hearing that, the slaughter began.

The raiders fired on everything—horses, dogs and men. Men were dragged from their beds, their hands tied behind their backs, and led outside. Many were shot in front of their families.

The list of atrocities on that day is long. Men were wounded, then thrown into a raging fire to die. Many were hanged. House by house, the raiders took over the town, setting fires and robbing soldiers and civilians alike.

Interestingly, no women were harmed. This was an order from Quantrill himself. Because of this, the bushwhackers of Missouri considered themselves better than the guerrillas from Kansas. James Lane and his band often killed women, and in the tragic collapse of the jail in Kansas City many women besides "Bloody Bill" Anderson's sisters were killed.

Historians say few wounded lived to tell the story of the attack on Lawrence. The raiders often repeatedly fired into piles of bodies, just in case one was alive.

One survivor was the man at the top of Quantrill's hate list—James Lane. When he heard the shooting and screaming, Lane rushed downstairs in his nightshirt. He took the name plate from his door, ran out his back door and hid in a cornfield.

The slaughter lasted about four hours. At nine o'clock that morning, two of Quantrill's lookouts saw Union troops approaching. The guerrillas fled back to Missouri.

In all, 150 men and boys were murdered. More than $2 million in damage was done. Hundreds of houses lay in ashes. Bones were visible among the embers, and the odor of burning flesh filled the air.

Union soldiers now regarded Quantrill and his

men as criminals. Generals gave orders to find and hang Quantrill and other bushwhackers.

NOT THROUGH YET

Quantrill and his men went to Texas later in 1863, raiding towns and wiping out entire patrols of Union soldiers. It is estimated that they killed at least 1,000 men in 1863.

In Texas the guerrillas disagreed about who should be in charge. Some left to form their own guerrilla bands. Others stayed with Quantrill.

Quantrill and the men loyal to him made raids in Missouri, Texas and other southern states before riding to Kentucky. There, in 1865, he was hunted down and killed, then buried in Louisville. Twenty years later, his mother asked for, received and sold his bones. No one knows to whom. It was an exchange that raised a fascinating question: Why would anyone buy them?

You have just read the known facts about one of HISTORY'S MYSTERIES. To date, there have been no more answers to the mysteries posed in the story. There are possibilities, though. Read on and see which answer seems the most believable to you. How would you solve the case?

SOLUTIONS

▲▲▲▲▲▲▲▲▲▲▲▲▲▲▲▲▲▲▲▲▲▲▲▲▲▲▲▲▲▲

HIDE A MONSTER

Many people called William Quantrill a "bloodthirsty monster." Together with his band of raiders, Quantrill was responsible for the deaths of hundreds of innocent people. He fought under a black flag, not a Confederate flag. His victims were not only soldiers, but also unarmed civilians.

Still, at one time or another, 450 men had followed Quantrill in the private war he fought for the proslavery movement. An abolitionist may have bought his bones to stop any chance that Quantrill's grave site would become a political memorial.

MAKE A SHRINE

The tension and hatred between those in Missouri and Kansas before the Civil War resulted in furious fighting. Crimes were committed in the name of each cause. There were guerrillas on the Union side too. They savagely killed and burned just as Quantrill and his men did. But the Union side won the war, and their fighters were not criticized.

Quantrill was vicious, but no more so than any other guerrilla fighters—and there were many. He and his band of raiders were Confederates, fighting for what they believed in. He was not a monster. He was simply a soldier fighting in a brutal war. One of his men, or another proslavery sympathizer, may have bought his bones to build a private shrine for comrades in arms or allies.

CLOSING THE CASE FILE

▲▲▲▲▲▲▲▲▲▲▲▲▲▲▲▲▲▲▲▲▲▲▲▲▲▲▲▲

It's difficult to judge the worth of any person, especially one who died as young as William Quantrill. There is no way to know what kind of person he might have become if he'd lived long after the war was over. He might have become an outlaw like his fellow raiders Frank and Jesse James and Cole Younger did. He might have become a respectable, law-abiding citizen like others of the raiders did.

The border war between Kansas and Missouri in the 1850s and 1860s was bloody and fierce. Soldiers fought violently, in order to survive.

A photograph taken in Independence, Missouri, in 1900 at a reunion of Quantrill's raiders shows a crowd of gray-haired men standing proudly at attention. As Michael Fellman wrote in *Inside War*, the guerrillas "had become just another group of

prosperous-looking, aging farmers and small-town merchants who had once been boys at war."

The idea is chilling. If Quantrill was a monster, then were these soldiers monsters too? Or was war the monster?

CHRONOLOGY

▲▲▲▲▲▲▲▲▲▲▲▲▲▲▲▲▲▲▲▲▲▲▲▲▲▲▲▲▲▲▲▲▲▲

1837   July 31, William Quantrill is born.

1854   Kansas-Nebraska Act is passed.

1855   July First free elections in Kansas Territory. Proslavery legislature is established in Pawnee Mission, Kansas.
October Abolitionist legislature is established in Lawrence, Kansas.

1857   Quantrill first arrives in Kansas.

1860   December Quantrill moves from Kansas to Missouri.

1861   January 29, Kansas wins statehood.
April 12, Civil War begins.

1862   Union outlaws Quantrill and raiders.

1863   Quantrill visits Confederate leaders.
August 21, Lawrence Massacre takes place.

1864   Union army kills "Bloody Bill"
        Anderson.

1865   May 10, Union patrol surprises Quantrill
                and raiders at Wakefield's farm.
        June 6, Quantrill dies.

1887   Quantrill's remains are exhumed and
        sold.

RESOURCES
▲▲▲▲▲▲▲▲▲▲▲▲▲▲▲▲▲▲▲▲▲▲▲▲▲▲▲▲▲▲▲▲▲▲▲▲▲

SOURCES

Brownlee, Richard S. *Gray Ghosts of the Confederacy*. Baton Rouge: Louisiana State University Press, 1958.

Connelly, William E. *Quantrill and the Border Wars*. Cedar Rapids, Ia.: Torch Press, 1910.

Nevins, Allan. *Ordeal of the Union*, Vol. II. New York: Charles Scribner's Sons, 1947.

FURTHER READING FOR
YOUNG READERS

Katz, William L. *An Album of the Civil War*. New York: Franklin Watts, 1974.

Miers, Earl S. *Billy Yank and Johnny Reb*. Chicago: Rand McNally, 1959.

Werstein, Irving. *The Many Faces of the Civil War*. New York: Julian Messner, 1961.

INDEX

▲▲